Contents

List of illustrations

Acknowledgements

I have been interested in pillow mounds, and in other aspects of the archaeology of rabbit warrens, for more than a quarter of a century, and during this time many people have provided me with information, help or encouragement. I would like to thank, in particular, David Austin, Mark Bailey, John Barnatt, Sarah Harrison, Catherine Hills, Rosemary Hoppitt, Robert Liddiard, Roy Loveday, Anne Mason, Ivan Ringwood, Anne Rowe, John Sheail, Robert Silvester, Christopher Taylor, Joan Thirsk and Angus Wainwright.

Thanks also to Tracey Rich/ARWP Ltd, for figure 1 (also on the front cover); to the Cambridge Committee for Aerial Photography, for permission to reproduce figures 5, 9, 16, 17, 18, 19 and 23; to Norfolk Records Office, for permission to reproduce figure 3 (also on the front cover); to the British Library, for permission to reproduce figure 2; to the Ancient House Museum, Thetford, for permission to reproduce figure 4; to Nicola Whyte, who supplied figure 44; and to Barry Cunliffe for figures 13 and 28. Philip Judge provided the maps and line drawings, and Rik Hoggett plotted figure 8, from information kindly supplied by the National Monuments Record, the Cambridge Committee for Aerial Photography, the Ordnance Survey archaeological records, and the various county Sites and Monuments Records. Above all, I would like to thank my family for their remarkable tolerance of an obsession which has blighted country walks and holidays over several decades.

1
Rabbits and rabbit farming

The rabbit (*Oryctolagus cuniculus*) existed in Britain before the last ice age but then died out (figure 1). There may have been attempts to reintroduce it during the Roman period but, so far as the evidence goes, the rabbit was unknown to the Anglo-Saxons and did not become successfully re-established until after the Norman Conquest. The earliest documentary record probably dates from 1135, when Drake's Island in Plymouth Sound was granted to Plympton Priory *cum cuniculi* ('with the rabbits'). Initially the coney (the word 'rabbit' was, until the eighteenth century, reserved for the young) was a domesticated or semi-domesticated animal, kept in special areas (figure 2). It was poorly adapted to the British climate and only gradually, as a result of natural selection, became the hardy wild animal we know today.

To begin with, rabbits were usually kept in relatively small enclosures or *coneygarths*, located close to castles, monasteries or manor houses,

1. The rabbit, *Oryctolagus cuniculus*, is today a common sight in the countryside but it was originally a semi-domesticated animal – an introduced alien which was poorly suited to the British environment.

2. Women catching rabbits with ferret and purse-net, from the fourteenth-century *Queen Mary's Psalter*. The low earth mound in which the rabbits are living is probably an artificial warren or 'pillow mound'.

and especially in deer parks. The few larger warrens were mainly on islands, where the animals could more easily be protected from predators. But by the thirteenth century large commercial warrens were appearing on the mainland, usually in sandy areas, often on the coast, but also inland. Rabbits were kept both for their fur and for their meat. They were luxury items: a single animal in the thirteenth century was worth more than a workman's daily wage.

Rabbit warrens seem to have increased in number during the late fourteenth and fifteenth centuries. As the population declined following the Black Death, and grain prices tumbled, rabbits represented a useful form of agricultural diversification for manorial lords. Warrens posed many management problems, not least because rabbits were vulnerable to disease: but the animals bred rapidly and were an extremely efficient way of utilising rough grazing. Many of the larger warrens, moreover, were located in areas of common land, and the law held that a manorial lord could introduce rabbits on to his waste without infringing or diminishing the common rights of his tenants. By the sixteenth century warrens were thus widespread not only in districts characterised by sandy heaths, such as the East Anglian Breckland (figure 3), but also in many areas of chalk downland, and in some forests, such as Savernake and Ashdown. During this period, indeed, rabbit numbers generally increased in the wild, especially in lowland districts, as the species became better adapted to the environment. By 1581 the German naturalist Gesner was able to comment on the 'great abundance' of rabbits in England and it is possible that some commercial warrens, in areas of lowland heath and

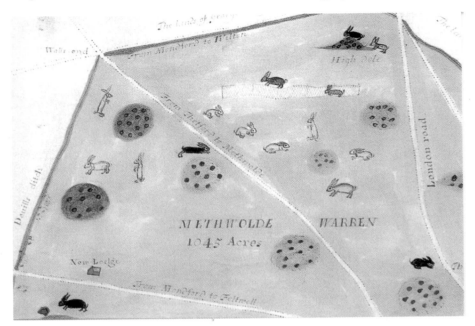

3. Methwold Warren in the Norfolk Breckland, as depicted on an estate map of 1699. As well as the rabbits themselves – some apparently of the black or 'muel' variety for which Methwold was well known – the map shows the warren boundaries, that to the north-west formed by the Dark Age earthwork called the Fossditch; the 'new lodge'; a long net or 'haye', used to catch the rabbits; and what are probably a number of 'buries' or pillow mounds.

downland especially, were actually established *after* rabbit populations had developed there naturally.

In the late medieval period, and into the sixteenth and seventeenth centuries, coneygarths continued to be a valued element of elite landscapes. Like dovecotes and fishponds, they were important symbols of status, to be proudly displayed beside the main approaches to the mansion, or carefully positioned on the skyline, to be viewed with pleasure from its windows. Some warrens may have had a deeper significance. Rabbits may now be best known for their breeding qualities but in medieval Christian iconography they carried other connotations. Small, defenceless, and under the protection of the warrener, emerging from underground darkness into the light – in a deeply symbolic world rabbits came to signify mankind and his salvation through Christ and the church. David and Margarita Stocker have noted how warrens are prominently displayed in the precincts of medieval monasteries like Sawtry Abbey, Cambridgeshire. The complex triangular warren lodge built at Rushton in Northamptonshire by the Catholic recusant Thomas Tresham in the 1590s – its three sides providing both a pun on Tresham's name and a statement of his faith in the Tridentine mass – was certainly a badge of allegiance to the old Catholic faith in post-Reformation England.

Most of the rabbits kept in warrens were of the common grey variety – the normal wild rabbit – but black rabbits were also kept, their skins in great demand as ornamental trimming for clothes. The silver-grey or silver-blue was also greatly valued: it was particularly associated with the warrens of the north-east of England but could be found more widely. The rabbits were born in May and June and normally killed between October and February, when their fur was fully developed, although on some warrens, where supplies of winter feed were restricted, culling might begin as early as late summer.

In the Middle Ages most warrens were directly administered by their owners as part of the demesne economy, but from the fifteenth century it became more usual to lease the larger ones out to professional warreners. The lease agreements usually state, in some detail, what was expected of the lessee, such as how many rabbits were to be left at the end of the tenancy. At Nacton in Suffolk, for example, the tenant was to leave 'five hundred couple of coneys good, well conditioned and alive' when the lease expired in 1646. The rent was often paid in part, and occasionally entirely, in rabbits. Leases also usually note that the various buildings and facilities on the warren should be maintained in good condition, and describe what equipment should be left at the end of the tenancy. They can thus be an important source of information about the field archaeology, and the material culture, of warrening. Not all post-medieval exploitation of rabbits, however, took the form of large commercial warrens or domestic enclosures. Rabbits were also caught on a regular, systematic but small-scale basis by farmers living in marginal areas, as a useful way of supplementing the income from more mainstream agricultural enterprises – a form of exploitation which has usefully been described as the 'farm warren'.

There were important changes in the management of warrens in the course of the later seventeenth and eighteenth centuries. Fodder crops seem to have been used on a larger scale in order to increase the numbers of rabbits that could be kept, especially through the autumn and winter. Hay, young bracken, gorse and brushwood had all been employed as feed in earlier times but, to judge from the available evidence, fodder now became more significant, particularly after turnips came into widespread use as a field crop from the late seventeenth century. But as stocking levels rose it became harder to keep the rabbits within the warren – in overcrowded conditions the young rabbits in particular were more prone to stray on to surrounding farmland – and this in turn made it more important to secure the warren boundary with some sort of rabbit-proof barrier, such as a wall or bank. Again, this was not an entirely new development. Small medieval coneygarths had usually been enclosed and even the larger warrens had often been surrounded, at least in part, by a bank and ditch. But the scale and extent of enclosure probably increased during the post-medieval period.

In the course of the eighteenth and nineteenth centuries rabbits gradually ceased to be an expensive, luxury item. Their price fell as they became more common, and they eventually became a food for the poor and a raw material for cheap items of clothing, especially hats. Along with fishponds, orchards and dovecotes, in the course of the eighteenth century warrens were cleared away from the vicinity of mansions and banished from parks. Yet at the same time large commercial warrens continued to be developed, especially in upland areas – on high moors – where they had formerly been rare. Most were established by large landed estates but some were created without permission. In 1760 the lessee of the Corwon lands at Maelienydd in Radnorshire (now Powys), for example, ordered his agents to destroy a warren in the parish of Llanddewi Ystradenni, 'dug for keeping rabbits, without licence or authority'. In

4. Warreners at North Farm, Barnham, Suffolk, in 1921, with their traditional equipment: dogs, long-handled staves and ferrets (in the boxes). Commercial warrens continued to function at several places in Breckland into the middle decades of the twentieth century.

the same period, warrens began to decline in importance in many of their traditional heartlands of downland, wolds and heath. During the later eighteenth century the new techniques of the agricultural revolution allowed the profitable cultivation of such areas of poor, light soil. Decline accelerated in these areas in the course of the nineteenth century. Landowners considered warrens and rabbit farming uncommercial and old-fashioned, and with an increasing abundance of other meat the market for rabbits dwindled.

Nevertheless, the decline of commercial warrens was gradual and uneven. New ones continued to appear during the nineteenth century in some upland districts, especially in Wales, where rabbits provided a ready source of cheap meat for nearby industrialising areas. They hung on into the twentieth century in some particularly marginal areas, such as Dartmoor, the Tabular Hills in North Yorkshire and the East Anglian Breckland. In certain districts warrens thrived because they provided raw materials for particular industries, such as hat-making in the Ribble valley in Lancashire. In Breckland, as late as the 1920s, nearly half the area of the Elveden estate near Thetford was given over to warrens: thirty warreners were employed and 120,000 rabbits were taken annually. Some of the warrens around Brandon continued to function into the 1950s, the rabbits being sold both for meat and for fur, the latter used in particular for making felt hats (figure 4). Only the advent of myxamotosis in 1954 finally brought this ancient Breckland industry to an end.

Warrens, especially the larger ones, were noticeable features of the landscape. They are often depicted on early maps and frequently gave their name to adjacent roads and fields. In areas of heathland, in particular, intense grazing gave them a distinctive, often desolate appearance. The rabbits stripped the turf, exposing the sand beneath to the force of the wind and leading to the formation of mobile dunes, like those which, blown out of Lakenheath Warren in Breckland, partly engulfed the village of Santon Downham in 1668 and blocked the river Little Ouse. Plants like clover and trefoil declined in abundance; nettles and the tougher grasses tended to flourish. But as well as being distinctive by virtue of their ecology and appearance, warrens also contained a number of characteristic structures (figure 5).

Firstly, as already noted, many warrens were surrounded by banks or walls, to prevent the rabbits from escaping. Escaped rabbits not only meant a loss of profit. They might cause damage to neighbouring crops, leading to prosecutions from other landowners. Many warrens also contained internal subdivisions and enclosures, similarly defined by walls or banks, sometimes to allow more efficient management of the grazing, sometimes to permit fodder crops to be cultivated, sometimes for other purposes.

Secondly, most of the larger warrens contained lodges or warren houses.

5. Aerial view of the former warren at Minchinhampton Common in the Gloucestershire Cotswolds. This is one of the largest surviving groups of pillow mounds in England and includes both round and rectangular examples. Many are 'segmented' – that is, cut by shallow surface grooves. The building at the end of the track is the former warren lodge, now a public house.

These served as a home and working base for the warrener and could be well-built, elaborate structures. The warrener needed to be resident in order to protect the rabbits from predators and, in particular, from poachers. Hungry peasants must have looked with envy at well-stocked warrens, but in the Middle Ages many convicted poachers came from more affluent sections of the community. In the early fifteenth century Augustinian canons from Blythburgh Priory in Suffolk were regularly convicted of poaching in the warren at Westwood near Dunwich: one, Thomas Sherman, was actually described in a court case of 1425 as 'a poaching canon'!

Thirdly, warrens were supplied with special traps to catch the various vermin that preyed on the rabbits, and these have sometimes left archaeological traces; so too have the rather larger traps which, on a minority of warrens, were used to catch the rabbits themselves. Lastly, and most importantly, on many warrens the rabbits were provided with purpose-built accommodation. This usually took the form of low, rectangular mounds, called 'pillow mounds' by archaeologists, but round mounds, cross-shaped mounds, mounds of irregular shape or earlier earthworks, specially adapted, were also used. All provided soft dry earth suitable for the rabbits to burrow in, and some were also specially designed to make it easier to trap the animals.

Warrens were a very common feature of the medieval and post-medieval landscape but they are, nevertheless, surprisingly poorly documented in the historical record. Even eighteenth- and nineteenth-century warrens are often known only from minor place-names or from a passing reference in estate accounts. This is one reason why the archaeological evidence for rabbit farming is of such importance. But in addition, some of the physical traces left by warrens – especially pillow mounds – have been systematically misinterpreted by archaeologists in the past, often as features of prehistoric or Roman date. This is partly because warrens often lay in areas of early settlement, but also because the mounds themselves were sometimes elaborate and complex in character, containing structures that unwary archaeologists have, on occasions, interpreted as the remains of buildings or as traces of past 'ritual' activity. For both these reasons – as well as for their intrinsic interest, as features of the historic landscape – the physical remains of rabbit warrens are worthy of serious attention.

2
The location and morphology
of pillow mounds

The most common of the archaeological remains left by warrening are the distinctive low mounds first termed 'pillow mounds' by O. G. S. Crawford in the 1920s. Crawford noticed them while making his pioneer forays into aerial archaeology (figure 6) but archaeologists had puzzled over their age and function for several decades. As early as 1879 Pitt-Rivers suggested that they were artificial rabbit accommodation, for he

6. This curious group of mounds on Steeple Langford Cowdown, in Wiltshire, was photographed from the air by a puzzled O. G. S. Crawford in the 1920s. It included pillow mounds of normal rectangular and circular form, but also some larger mounds: all displayed considerable evidence of 'segmenting'.

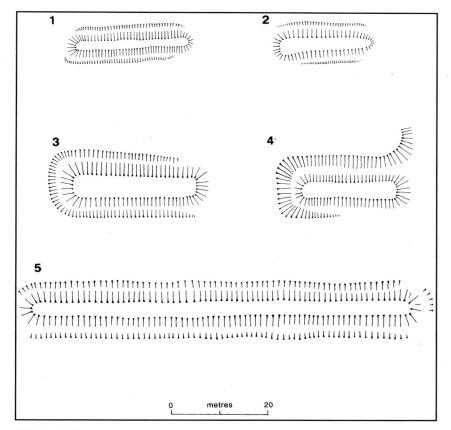

7. Typical pillow mounds. Pillow mounds can vary greatly in length, while seldom exceeding a width of about 10 metres. 1, Llanelwedd, Powys (after RCAHM, Wales); 2, Penmaen Burrows, Glamorgan (after RCAHM, Wales); 3, Cwm Ednant, Darowen, Powys; 4, Stoke Doyle, Northamptonshire (after RCHME); 5, Hartfield, East Sussex (after Ordnance Survey Archaeological Records).

had seen examples still being used for this purpose on Dartmoor. But many archaeologists remained unconvinced, not least because – as Crawford himself noted – pillow mounds were often found in areas of dry, light soil where 'such temptations to burrow seem rather superfluous'. The 'rabbit warren' explanation has gradually become accepted but much about the form and function of these earthworks continues to confuse.

In some ways Crawford's choice of name was unsatisfactory. The mounds do not usually resemble a pillow in the modern sense, but rather an old-fashioned bolster, long and thin in shape. But, in addition, it is

clear that there was a common vernacular term for these features: they
were called 'buries', 'berries' or 'burrows', and leases for warrens often
insisted that they should be kept in good repair. Either way, pillow mounds
may be defined as approximately rectangular mounds of equal height
and width throughout, usually a metre or less in height, and with a flanking
ditch which – unlike those associated with Neolithic long barrows –
usually runs all the way around the mound, rather than only along the
sides (figure 7). Some mounds (especially in the lowlands) have ends
that are neat and square; others have ones that are less regular and/or
more rounded in plan. Many mounds, and again especially those found
in lowland districts, are relatively flat-topped, but in upland areas profiles
are often more ridged and the mounds are usually higher: the distinction
is not absolute, but evident nevertheless. In upland areas, moreover, the
sides of the perimeter ditches may be retained by dry-stone walling, and
large slabs of stone are sometimes placed along the sides of the mound.
The smallest mounds can be less than 6 metres in length but the largest
can reach 150 metres. Few mounds, however, have a width greater than
10 metres, and the majority have transverse dimensions of between 4
and 8 metres. This, perhaps, is the most important defining characteristic
of a pillow mound.

Pillow mounds can occur in level situations but are more common on
sloping ground, where they are usually orientated roughly at right angles
to the contours. They can occur singly, or in groups containing anything
up to ninety examples. Mounds are sometimes conjoined – that is,
arranged end-to-end in such a way that two or more share the same
ditches. They can form a long line, as at High Beach in Essex; an open
polygon, as at Hartfield in East Sussex; or even a square, as at Pilsdon
Pen in Dorset.

There are well over two thousand individual pillow mounds recorded
in England and Wales, in over five hundred distinct groups. As figure 8
shows, most have been noted in the west, especially on the moorlands of
Wales, Devon and Cornwall, in the Cotswolds, and on the chalk
downlands of Wessex. Up to a point this distribution is the consequence
of later land-use patterns – of the greater extent and intensity of arable
farming in the east, and the consequent destruction of these relatively
slight features by later ploughing. Documentary evidence certainly
suggests that pillow mounds were once common in districts where they
are now rare or absent. There are thus only a handful of surviving
examples in the county of Norfolk but in 1596, during a court case
concerning an area of heathland in the parish of Swainsthorpe, the judge
enquired whether there were 'any great highe burrowes upon the said
pece of ground such as be commonly in warrens' and the witness was
able to reply: 'Yea my lorde.' Yet the western bias in the distribution of

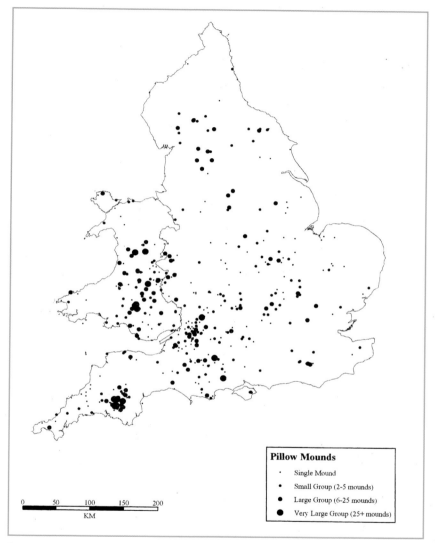

8. The distribution of known pillow mounds in England and Wales. (Source: RCHME, RCAHM, Ordnance Survey Archaeological Records, Cambridge University Aerial Photography Library, county Sites and Monuments Records/Historic Environment Records)

mounds is probably not *only* the consequence of such factors. It is noticeable that most of the largest groups of mounds are recorded in the west (and to some extent the north) of Britain, suggesting that the impetus for their construction was greatest there. On the high moorlands of central and southern Wales there are several very large concentrations, with groups of over fifty at Cray and nearly ninety at Ystradfellte in the Brecon Beacons. These have a number of associated features, including walled enclosures, ruined buildings and stone-lined trapping pits. Particularly large concentrations of mounds are also a feature of Dartmoor, again

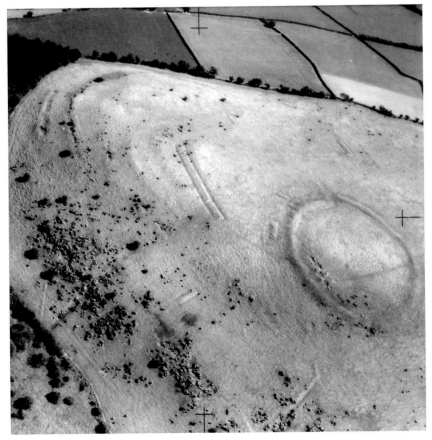

9. A group of pillow mounds at Llanspyddid, Powys, typically situated on open moorland (now afforested) and close to the earthworks of an Iron Age enclosure.

associated with enclosures and warren houses. There are some notable groups in the Cotswolds, especially at Minchinhampton, and on the Wessex downs. But few really large concentrations are known from elsewhere in the lowlands of the south and east, and on the whole rather smaller groups, or even single mounds, are the norm here, frequently unassociated with any other obvious evidence of warrening activity. Moreover, many warrens in the south and east, located in areas which have not subsequently been much ploughed – such as the East Anglian Breckland – seem to have had few or no pillow mounds, and evidently functioned well enough without them.

In a number of ways pillow mounds display a measure of local variation – they have, as it were, their own regional personalities. Sussex and Surrey mounds, for example, are distinguished by their considerable length: most are more than 50 metres long, and some as much as 150 metres. In south Wales there is a clear distinction between the compact mounds, in small groups, found near the coast and the large concentrations of often more substantial mounds, associated with their ruined buildings and enclosures, found on the inland moors.

Two general aspects of the mounds' location are worthy of note. The first is that a very high proportion – probably around two-thirds – are found in areas which are still, or were until enclosure in the eighteenth or nineteenth century, common land. The second is their close association with earlier earthworks. Many mounds are found within or beside Iron Age hillforts (figure 9) or beside Bronze Age round barrows: some examples are actually built into the sides of such features. At Alton Barnes in Wiltshire, for example, two probable pillow mounds are inserted into the sides of a long barrow, while in Hatfield Forest in Essex a chain of mounds appears to have been created by adapting an earlier, perhaps prehistoric, enclosure.

A large number of pillow mounds have been excavated, often under the impression that they were barrows. Some, like those at Everage Clough, Burnley, Lancashire, were found to be of simple dump construction, formed of layers of earth dug from the encircling ditch (figure 10), although examples at Sutton-in-Craven in North Yorkshire and Hollybush Hill in Herefordshire also contained material brought to the site from a distance. Other excavated mounds, however, have proved to be more complex. Many upland examples contain large or medium-sized stones, sometimes arranged in an amorphous fashion at the base of the mound, as at Lanlivery in Cornwall, but often forming distinct patterns. A mound excavated at Llanelwedd near Builth Wells, Powys, in the 1960s thus overlay three lines of stones which ran the length of the mound, with short transverse lines branching off them and curious fan-like arrangements at the ends; another mound here, less extensively

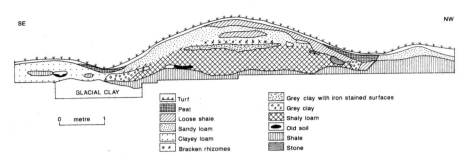

10. Cross-section of a typical pillow mound at Burnley in Lancashire, excavated by T. Seddon and F. Willett in the early 1950s (and published in *Transactions of the Lancashire and Cheshire Antiquaries Society* for 1953). The mound was of simple dump construction, apparently without internal features.

excavated, covered similar lines. Mounds at Cefn Hirgoed in Glamorgan overlay slightly more regular arrangements, while a mixture of long lines, running the lengths of the mound and with short transverse branches, and more complex patterns, was discovered beneath the mounds at Llanfair Clydogau in Ceredigion (figure 11). At Castell Odo in Gwynedd, in contrast, the mound covered a single line of stones laid out along its axis. Other stone arrangements are described, or hinted at, in excavation reports from other sites, such as Bury Hill near Bristol, and they have sometimes been revealed where mounds have been partially destroyed, as at Mynydd Gelliwion near Pontypridd.

The amorphous masses of stone were probably intended simply to create spaces which would encourage burrowing. The more organised stone lines, in contrast, formed the capping for artificial burrows, something that David Austin first demonstrated by meticulous excavation at Llanfair Clydogau. Here the stones covered gullies dug into the old ground surface beneath the mound to a depth of about 20 cm. In areas where large stones are less readily available such artificial accommodation has left rather different traces – networks of simple slots cut into the subsoil. A number were excavated by Barry Cunliffe within the hillfort at Danebury in Hampshire, although the overlying mounds themselves had presumably been removed in the seventeenth century, when the interior of the fort was ploughed (figures 12 and 13). Similar features were revealed during the excavation of four mounds, arranged to form a square, within another hillfort – Pilsdon Pen in Dorset (figure 14). At both sites most of the slots were straight-sided, regular in shape and dug into the chalk to a depth of 20–30 cm. In some cases there was

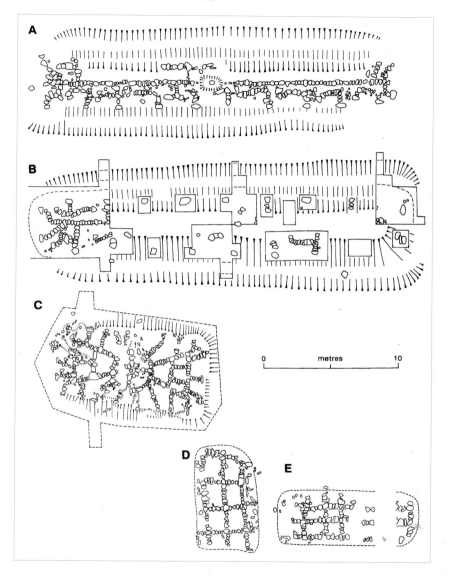

11. Lines of stones, often forming complex patterns, have been discovered beneath a number of excavated mounds, especially in Wales. The stones capped artificial burrows, dug into the old ground surface. A and B, Llanelwedd, near Builth Wells, Powys (after RCAHM); C, Llanfair Clydogau, Ceredigion (after David Austin); D and E, Cefn Hirgoed, Glamorgan (after RCAHM).

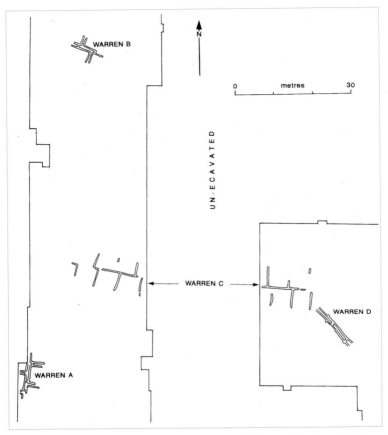

12. These slots, cut into the chalk within the Iron Age hillfort at Danebury in Hampshire, formed artificial burrow systems. They were probably covered by pillow mounds, levelled when the interior of the fort was ploughed in the seventeenth century. (After B. Cunliffe)

a long single slot, with shorter slots running off it at intervals; in others there were two parallel slots, linked by transverse slots and again with branches running out at right angles. Striations formed by animal claws were observed in the base of some of the Danebury slots: Cunliffe correctly concluded that 'The simplest suggestion is that the structures were created as artificial burrows to encourage rabbits'. Similar slots were discovered cut into the chalk beneath the large pillow mound on Sharpenhoe Clapper in Bedfordshire.

13. Parallel linear slots forming one of the artificial burrow systems within Danebury hillfort (the other features are of Iron Age date).

Of particular interest in this context are the mounds excavated by Robert Silvester at Y Foel, Llanllugan, in Powys (figure 15). These were built of an orange loam, derived from the subsoil, but were 'riddled with burrows filled with slightly sticky, loose humic soil'. Beneath two of the mounds straight, evidently artificial burrows were discovered, cut into the old ground surface. These had subsequently been augmented by the rabbits themselves, producing a less ordered pattern. It is not entirely clear what material was used to cap the original, artificial burrows here or, indeed, at the English sites just discussed. Silvester suggested 'turves, rushes, or some other organic material' which would 'now be difficult to detect archaeologically'. He also suggested that the mounds containing

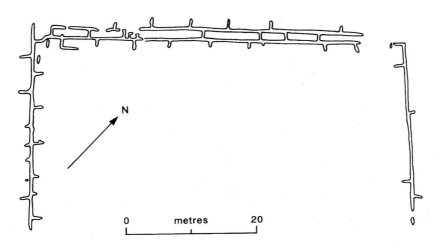

14. A complex of artificial burrows revealed when a group of conjoined pillow mounds within the hillfort at Pilsdon Pen in Dorset was excavated in the 1970s. The networks of slots were originally interpreted as the remains of an Iron Age 'ritual' building. (After P. Gelling)

artificial burrows may have been the first to be constructed on Y Foel, the original 'colonists' thus being provided with 'fully furnished residences', while their descendants made do with less sophisticated accommodation.

Not all artificial burrows were cut into the ground surface *beneath* the mound. Some seem to have been constructed within the body of the mound itself. Over the years these have settled and collapsed, giving rise to the phenomenon Crawford termed 'segmenting' – patterns of shallow surface grooves. These are most obvious from the air but are sometimes evident on the ground, as at Minchinhampton in Gloucestershire, where some of the mounds have grooves around 30 cm wide and as much as 40 cm deep. Segmenting takes a variety of forms. Some mounds have a single longitudinal groove, others varying numbers of transverse grooves, while some have both (figures 16 and 17). Their layout is often irregular and haphazard. Grooves often run at a skewed angle across the width of the mound and frequently do not lie precisely parallel with each other. Not all pillow mounds contained constructed burrows, although many evidently did so. In some cases rudimentary burrows were simply bored into the mound after its construction. Thus during Henry VIII's reign the household accounts for Hampton Court refer to the purchase of 'a great long auger of irne, to make and bore

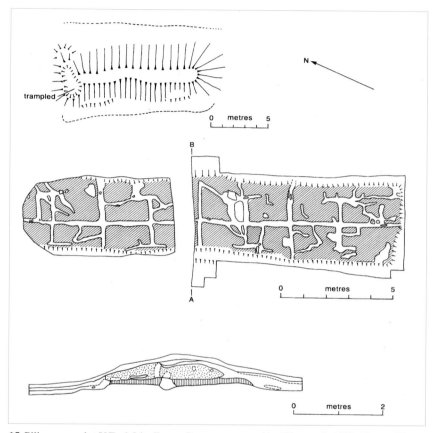

15. Pillow mound at Y Foel, Llanllugan, Powys, excavated by Silvester in 1990. The rectilinear character of the original artificial burrows, cut into the subsoil beneath the mound, contrasts with the more irregular pattern added by the rabbits themselves. (After R. Silvester)

cony holes within the kynges beries new made for blake conyes in the warren'.

The frequent association of pillow mounds with prehistoric earthworks, together with the presence within or beneath them of stone lines and linear slots, has led to much archaeological confusion. Indeed, it is probable that no other kind of field monument has been so consistently misunderstood by excavators. In the late nineteenth and early twentieth centuries, before the general acceptance of the 'rabbit warren' explanation, particular mounds were interpreted as boundary markers

16. Pillow mound at Houghton Conquest, Bedfordshire, with a single lengthways groove – traces of a collapsed burrow created within (rather than beneath) the mound.

for Roman estates, as the sites of Iron Age funeral pyres, as ritual structures of Dark Age date, and as Roman military buildings. Even after the widespread recognition that the mounds were built to accommodate rabbits, confusion continued, with several excavated examples in the 1940s and 1950s, such as those at Shute Shelve near Axbridge, Somerset, being interpreted as barrows. As late as 1969 the Royal Commission on Ancient and Historical Monuments in Wales, having excavated a mound at Llanelwedd in Powys containing not only stone lines but also quantities of Neolithic pottery, entertained for a short while the possibility that 'Though most pillow mounds must be artificial rabbit warrens ... some long low mounds indistinguishable from them are, in fact, a type of Neolithic burial mound'. At Pilsdon Pen in Dorset in the 1970s the four pillow mounds arranged in a square in the centre of

17. Pillow mound near the hillfort on Carregwiber Bank, Llandrindod Wells, Powys, displaying faint irregular transverse grooves.

the hillfort were interpreted as 'ritual structures', and the complex of slots uncovered beneath them as the sleeper beam trenches for an earlier timber-framed building, arranged around a central courtyard. The unparalleled rectilinear layout suggested Roman influence, while the extremely narrow spaces defined by the slots were considered storerooms as they seemed 'unsuitable for any obvious kind of human activity'. More famous, perhaps, is the mound at Crickley Hill, Gloucestershire. Interpreted by its excavator as a Neolithic bank barrow, this overlay a complex pattern of slots cut into the subsoil, contained mixed, topsoil-like material brought to the site from elsewhere and had large stone slabs placed at intervals along its sides – all classic pillow mound features. Conversely, in at least one case excavation has shown that an earthwork previously interpreted as a prehistoric feature was in reality a pillow mound. The narrow bank running transversely across a chalk spur at Sharpenhoe Clapper in Bedfordshire was widely considered to be an Iron Age rampart until excavations by Brian Dix in 1979 showed that it was of medieval or post-medieval date, and evidently a rather large pillow mound (the name 'Clapper' was a helpful clue: the Middle English word *clapere* means 'warren').

3
The age and purpose of pillow mounds

It is sometimes suggested that pillow mounds are medieval features but the archaeological and documentary evidence suggests that most surviving examples are of post-medieval date. True, it is often difficult to date individual mounds by excavation. Warrens were often established in remote, marginal locations, far from habitation, and mounds therefore contain little if any contemporary debris, although they sometimes produce residual material of prehistoric or Roman date. Conversely, material much *later* than the date of a mound's construction might be incorporated by the burrowing activities of the rabbits themselves. In 1925 the aptly named Hazeldine Warren, while excavating the mounds at High Beach in Epping Forest, noted that they contained 'a large amount of the debris of the present-day tripper', including 'high heels from shoes'! In spite of such problems, a number of excavations have produced reasonably convincing dating evidence, in the form of artefacts apparently incorporated within mounds during their construction. Finds made during the excavation of a mound at Charlcombe in Somerset in 1911 thus included the bowl of a clay tobacco pipe, and at Lanlivery in Cornwall sherds of late medieval pottery and pieces of coal were recovered, while the mounds excavated by Francis Villy in the 1920s at Sutton-in-Craven, North Yorkshire, produced forty sherds of medieval pottery, an eighteenth-century trade token and a George II halfpenny. At Everage Clough, Burnley, Lancashire, the excavators commented that the 'superficiality of the ditches ... is suggestive of a fairly recent origin', while the quantities of Scots pine pollen recovered from within one of the mounds suggest a post-medieval date, for this species of tree died out in the locality in Roman times and was not reintroduced until the seventeenth century. A pillow mound excavated on Rockford Common near Ellingham in Hampshire was found to overlie the bank of an enclosure which was itself of post-medieval date, and surface observation has similarly shown that many mounds are superimposed upon late medieval or post-medieval earthworks.

A number thus overlie 'ridge and furrow', the wave-like corrugations representing the plough ridges of former open fields (as at Croydon-cum-Clopton in Cambridgeshire, Edenham in Lincolnshire, Aston Sandford and Wing in Buckinghamshire, Babcary in Somerset, Little Sodbury in Gloucestershire (figure 18), Benefield in Northamptonshire, Markenfield Hall in North Yorkshire and Heytesbury in Wiltshire). Others overlie 'narrow rig', the diminutive form of ridge and furrow which

18. Little Sodbury, Gloucestershire. This large group of pillow mounds, some of unusual form, clearly overlies medieval or later 'ridge and furrow'.

normally dates from the eighteenth or early nineteenth century (as at Y Foel, Llanllugan; Llandegley (figure 19); and Cwm Ednant, Darowen, all in Powys; or on Skaigh Moor, Dartmoor). A number are superimposed on the earthworks of late medieval settlement desertion (as at Doddington or Ham Hill in Somerset), while at Black Knoll, Plowden, Shropshire, two mounds overlie post-medieval hollow ways.

In fairness, it should be noted that – given the slight dimensions of many pillow mounds and their consequent vulnerability to destruction – the reverse situation (of ridge and furrow, for example, overlying a mound) is unlikely to be observed, although there is one possible example of this particular relationship at Sulby in Northamptonshire. Nevertheless, the general appearance of most mounds suggests relative modernity. In the 1920s the archaeologist Cyril Fox commented on those in Glamorgan that:

> A marked and consistent feature is their perfect condition. The ditches are always complete, frequently lacking that smoothness of profile which great age gives to earthwork. On the other hand, they are old enough to have accumulated a sufficient depth of humus to present the same flora as that of the adjacent undisturbed ground, and therefore have no obvious indications of modernity.

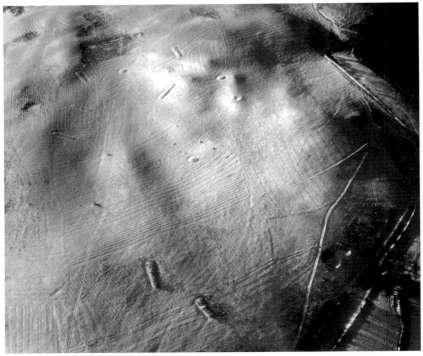

19. Llandegley, Powys. A group of mounds, including both circular and rectangular examples, which partly overlies 'narrow rig' – probably representing arable cultivation during the Napoleonic Wars.

On the basis of these characteristics, which are shared by most pillow mounds in Britain, Fox suggested that the Glamorgan examples were 'not earlier than late medieval'.

Documentary and cartographic evidence associates many pillow mounds with warrens of post-medieval date. At Rockingham in Northamptonshire, for example, a group of mounds lies within a warren created in 1616; at Weekley in the same county a single mound lies within an area called 'The Warren' on seventeenth-century maps; at Edensor in Derbyshire several lie within an area described as 'Conygarth' on Senior's 1617 survey of the Chatsworth estate; while at Hartfield in East Sussex two separate groups of mounds occur in areas referred to as 'The Warren' and 'Warren Lodge' in a Parliamentary survey of 1646. It is, of course, probable that some at least of these warrens had already existed in medieval times, but elsewhere the evidence for a post-medieval date is less equivocal. The warren slots excavated by Cunliffe at Danebury, for example, lay within an area described in 1678 as 'anciently and till since the memory of man a warren', but this had begun life only in the sixteenth century, when the area in question ceased to be used as the site for a fair (Cunliffe recovered a single sherd of post-medieval pottery from one of the slots). While some of the groups of pillow mounds on Dartmoor, such as those at Trowlesworthy and Ditsworthy, seem to be associated with medieval warrens most lie within ones with sixteenth-century or later origins. The various groups of mounds on the moorlands of southern and central Wales have, on the basis of circumstantial evidence, been plausibly dated to the eighteenth or early nineteenth century, not least because agricultural writers and others make it clear that the rabbit was virtually unknown in the interior of that country before this time. The large mound groups at Ystradfellte and Cray in Powys lie within part of the Great Forest of Brecknock which was not sold off by the Crown until 1820 (figure 20).

Occasionally, we can even identify the individual landowners responsible for the erection of particular mounds. Those in Hatfield Forest in Essex are almost certainly the 'Coney Burroughs' which Lord Morley

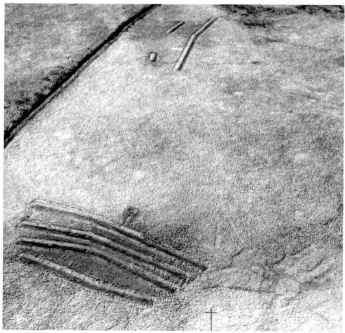

20. Part of a large group of very regular mounds at Ystradfellte in Powys, which is probably of early nineteenth-century date, post-dating the enclosure of Brecknockshire Forest in 1819. There are several other large warrens in the Brecon Beacons which are almost certainly of similar vintage.

constructed in the 1640s, and for which he was repeatedly fined in his own manorial court; while, according to estate records, the mounds at Trelleck in Monmouthshire were erected some time before 1719 by the landowner, one Colonel Henry Probert.

Indeed, documentary and oral evidence suggests that pillow mounds continued to be constructed, as well as utilised, well into the second half of the nineteenth century. At Walford in Herefordshire Ordnance Survey archaeologists were informed in 1958 by local people that a group of four mounds had been constructed only seventy years earlier, while at High Beach in Essex in 1925 the excavator's interpretation of the mounds as prehistoric ritual structures was made in the face of local opinion: 'Several old inhabitants of unimpeachable veracity are confident that the mounds were made within their own memory to serve the purpose of artificial rabbit warrens.'

While the available evidence thus suggests that most surviving pillow mounds were built between *c*.1550 and 1850, there is no doubt that they were a common enough feature of medieval warrens. What certainly appears to be an example is illustrated in the fourteenth-century *Queen Mary's Psalter* (figure 2) and examples are found in a number of places where medieval warrens are documented. The mound on Barry Island, Glamorgan, for example, lies within the area of a warren mentioned in 1491, while an example in the park at Castle Combe, Wiltshire, is probably associated with the warren which was leased here in 1416 (this is one of several mounds associated with parks with probable late fourteenth- or fifteenth-century origins). Other mounds are associated with the earthworks of medieval monastic precincts with which they appear to be contemporary (as at Isleham and Sawtry in Cambridgeshire, and Bruton in Somerset). The pillow mounds excavated at Llanfair Clydogau in Ceredigion by David Austin produced fragments of charcoal giving radiocarbon dates centring on the fourteenth century, although it is just possible that these were related to fires made in the area long before the mound's construction. Above all, there are a number of references to 'buries' and 'burrows' in texts from the sixteenth century which imply that they were by then well-established, normal features of the landscape. When Thomas Tusser wrote his *Five Hundred Pointes of Good Husbandrie* in 1573, for example, his advice for January included the injunction to 'Spare labour nor monie/store borough with conie'.

While there is no doubt that pillow mounds were constructed to provide accommodation for rabbits, it is not immediately apparent why the creatures should have required this, nor indeed why warreners needed to build mounds of this particular and distinctive form. The primary purpose of the mounds was, however, clearly to provide a raised area of loose, dry soil in which the rabbits could burrow. Rabbits prefer to make their homes on sloping ground, for in such circumstances the excavated soil falls away easily from the mouth of the hole. Moreover, they need well-drained soil and fail to thrive in damp conditions, and their young, in particular, are very vulnerable to drowning. The ditch surrounding the mound would have helped to keep the burrows dry, and drainage would have been further assisted by the fact that most mounds are orientated, as we have seen, roughly at right angles to the contours. On Dartmoor in the early twentieth century earth and peat were periodically dug from the ditches and piled on top of the 'buries' by the warreners, who insisted on the importance of keeping the 'roof' intact. Entry was restricted to lateral burrows, for otherwise the mound would become damp or waterlogged. Excavations carried out on a number of mounds – such as those at Everage Clough in Lancashire, and at Sutton-in-Craven in North Yorkshire – have revealed marked layers of soil which may represent successive attempts to maintain the 'roof'. Elsewhere – at Axbridge in Somerset and at Castell Odo in Gwynedd, for example – the stone 'cappings' to the mounds discovered during excavation probably represent attempts to discourage burrows emerging on the upper surface of the mound. In addition, leases suggest that vegetation was often laid on the surface of the mounds in the winter, partly to provide food for the rabbits but also to help keep them dry. One for the warren at Mildenhall in Wiltshire, drawn up in 1586, thus gave the tenant the right 'to cutt frythe [brushwood] to stragge [cover] the berryes' when the weather was poor. Another, of mid-sixteenth-century date, for the warren at Tyttenhanger in Hertfordshire, similarly refers to the tenant's right to take wood from the adjacent heath to 'cover, plash and lay the burrows'.

Looked at in this way, the distinctive, narrow, ditched form of the typical pillow mound makes immediate sense. Such a mound could easily be kept watertight, for material dug from the ditch (or brought from elsewhere) could be spread without difficulty right across its surface, by men standing on either side. In lowland warrens, maintenance of the rain-proof 'roof' was less important than in the damp uplands, and this may explain why pillow mounds in the latter areas tend to be higher, and to have more rounded profiles, than the lower, neater and generally flat-topped examples found in the south and east (figures 21 and 22).

In the uplands of northern and western Britain, where soils are often thin or waterlogged and rainfall is high, it might be necessary to provide purpose-built accommodation for most or even all of the rabbits on a warren, and it is here, as we have seen, that the largest groups of pillow mounds are to be found (figure 23). In more hospitable locations, in contrast, warreners mainly seem to have built mounds when new populations were being established on areas of heath, downland or other 'waste', or to house the most vulnerable members of

21. A Dartmoor pillow mound, displaying the high-backed form and rounded ends typical of mounds found in the uplands of England and Wales.

22. This pillow mound at Croydon-cum-Clopton in Cambridgeshire has the low profile, flat top and neat, squared ends often displayed by examples in lowland locations.

23. Aerial view of pillow mounds on Huntingdon Warren, Dartmoor. The largest groups of mounds are generally found, as here, on upland moors, presumably because in such bleak terrain it was necessary to provide accommodation for the entire population of the warren.

the rabbit population – the young and the breeding does. The Middle English term *clapere*, originally used for rabbit warrens in general, seems in later years to have been applied more narrowly, to special places where the does bred. John Lydgate's *Secrets of Old Philosoffies*, written in the early fifteenth century, thus describes how 'Yonge Rabbettys be to ther Claperys ronne', and it is probable that this term was by then employed for these breeding mounds, although it was also used for special hutches in which breeding does were kept.

Yet even in dry lowland areas with deep sandy soils warreners were sometimes prepared to build large numbers of mounds, as at High Beach in Epping Forest. Here the mounds excavated by Hazeldine Warren in 1925 – members of a group containing no less than twenty mounds – were still infested with rabbits, for 'the whole area [is] an exceptionally favourable one for them: it is all like a natural bank of dry Bagshot sand,

and the rabbits burrow in the natural surface quite freely ... The site
would certainly be a rabbit warren even if the mounds were not there.'
In areas of chalk downland, where soils are often thin, there might have
been more need to provide suitable accommodation, but here attention
should be drawn once again to the frequent association of pillow mounds
with earlier earthworks, such as barrows and hillforts. These monuments
often provided ready supplies of loose soil and rubble in which rabbits
could easily have made their homes. As Crawford noted in 1927, the
construction of pillow mounds in locations like these is, indeed,
superficially perplexing.

The explanation is probably that it was simply more convenient to
house rabbits in pillow mounds than to let them develop their own burrow
systems. Although rabbits were, on some warrens, caught in large pit
traps called 'types' (see page 53) they were usually taken with some
combination of ferrets, dogs and nets. Rabbits would be chased into
long nets or 'hays' erected at night between the burrows and their food:
concentrating the rabbits in a long, straight-sided mound obviously
facilitated such a procedure. But such mounds would also be a boon if
rabbits were being bolted by ferrets into individual purse-nets, placed
across the exit holes (figure 2). In a natural burrow system it is often
difficult to locate, and net, all of these and thus a proportion of the rabbits
invariably escape. The ferret, too, may make an unauthorised exit and
subsequently become a nuisance, difficult to recapture or kill. In addition,
natural warrens often contain a number of deep and exitless burrows
from which the rabbits refuse to bolt, and from which ferret and prey
might be recovered only after many hours of laborious digging. Such
difficulties could be reduced by encouraging the rabbits to dwell in a
mound which was both easy to net and from which they could be easily
bolted. A low, relatively narrow mound would contain few exitless
burrows, while the surrounding ditch – generally dug down to the level
of the hard subsoil or underlying rock – would serve to contain the burrow
system within the mound and thus reduce the possibility that rabbits
might escape from unlocated holes. The relatively short burrows
constructed, or developing naturally, within such a mound would
encourage rapid bolting. Once again, careful maintenance was necessary,
in order to ensure that the burrow system did not spread beneath the
ditch, and there is some evidence that, when it did, warreners would
break up the ground around the mounds by ploughing. A lease for a
warren at Cobham in Surrey, drawn up in 1647, thus stipulated that the
tenant should not destroy or dig down any of the rabbit burrows 'except
outholes by ploughing of the ground'.

The fact that pillow mounds were built for a variety of reasons means
that there is no very close relationship between the size or number of

mounds found on a particular warren and the size of the latter's population. Single mounds, or small groups, might represent 'clappers', or accommodation for a small pioneer population, on a large warren – like those scattered examples found on the vast warrens in the East Anglian Breckland and the Suffolk Sandlings; or they might represent attempts to house a much higher proportion of the population on a smaller warren. It is also likely that some small groups of mounds, and single examples, had a slightly different purpose: the small-scale, casual exploitation of scattered populations of essentially wild rabbits, by concentrating them in easily nettable mounds. At Hawkesbury in Gloucestershire local inhabitants informed Ordnance Survey archaeologists in the 1960s that a group of mounds had been constructed 'to attract rabbits'.

Whatever the precise motives for building particular mounds, regular maintenance of the 'roof' and the ditches presumably explains the remarkably neat and tidy appearance exhibited by many examples, a feature which has, somewhat paradoxically, often been considered incompatible with their function as rabbit accommodation. But it is interesting to note how we are forced to speculate in this way on the purpose and function of these enigmatic earthworks. Although the majority appear to be of post-medieval date and many remained in use into the nineteenth or even twentieth century, no surviving agricultural text or treatise on estate management tells us anything in detail about them, although several refer in passing to their existence.

4
Other forms of accommodation

Rectangular pillow mounds were not the only form of shelter and accommodation provided for rabbits on medieval and post-medieval warrens. Occasionally, as at Higham Ferrers in Northamptonshire, amorphous, irregularly shaped mounds were used. But more important were variant forms of carefully constructed 'bury'. As already noted, pillow mounds can sometimes be conjoined – that is, arranged in such a way that they are joined end to end, sharing the same ditches, so as to form curving lines, open polygons or squares. In some cases, the mounds themselves took such shapes (figure 24). At Winterbourne in Berkshire, for example, a mound forms three sides of a square while slightly V-shaped mounds have been recorded, as at Ystradfellte in Powys, and L-shaped examples, as at Llanfair Clydogau in Ceredigion. More importantly, at Mynydd Brombil near Port Talbot and at Merthyr Tydfil in Glamorgan, at Newport and Hayscastle in Pembrokeshire, at Chirbury in Shropshire, Banwell in Somerset, Swinton in Yorkshire and elsewhere cross-shaped mounds are found, a class of monument which for a while was given its own name by antiquarians – 'embanked crosses' (figure 25). These were the subject of much speculation in the past and even today

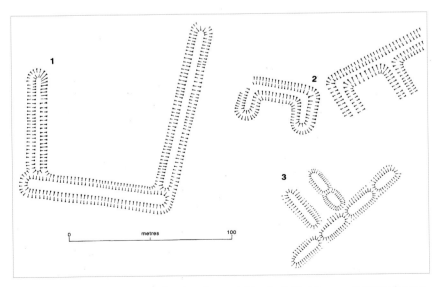

24. Conjoined pillow mounds and variant forms. 1, Hartfield, East Sussex; 2, Winterbourne, Berkshire; 3, High Beach, Epping Forest, Essex.

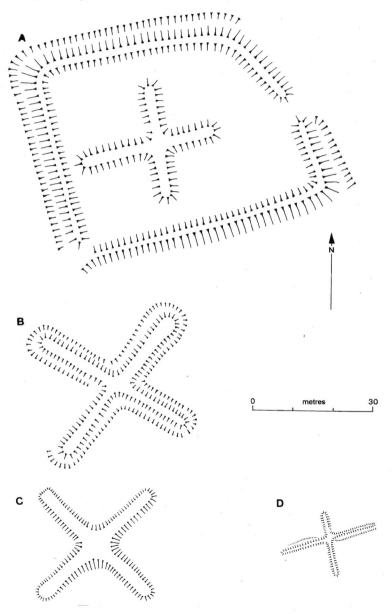

25. 'Embanked crosses' or cross-shaped pillow mounds. A, Banwell, Somerset; B, Chirbury, Shropshire; C, Mynydd Brombil, Port Talbot, Glamorgan; D, Merthyr Tydfil, Glamorgan.

sometimes cause confusion. That at Banwell, which lies within a rectangular enclosure (probably contemporary, perhaps an earlier feature), is interpreted by some as a memorial raised by Dark Age monks to commemorate the birthplace of St Patrick! But there is little doubt that most, if not all, of these monuments are unusual versions of pillow mounds. That at Port Talbot lies close to, and that at Chirbury lies beside, pillow mounds of normal form, while the former, when excavated in 1852, was found to overlie the by now familiar lines of stones.

Round mounds are a feature of many pillow mound groups – around a fifth contain some circular examples – and they occasionally occur without rectangular mounds. They are usually between 5 and 15 metres in diameter, although occasionally much larger – such as those, now destroyed, recorded by Crawford on Steeple Langford Cowdown in Wiltshire (figure 6). Like rectangular mounds, round examples usually have well-defined ditches and relatively sharp profiles, and some examples exhibit clear signs of 'segmenting', sometimes with a single lateral groove, more often with two set at right angles, meeting at the centre of the mound – an arrangement which Crawford in the 1920s christened the 'hot cross bun' form (figures 26 and 27). Round pillow

26. An example of a segmented circular pillow mound on Minchinhampton Common, Gloucestershire.

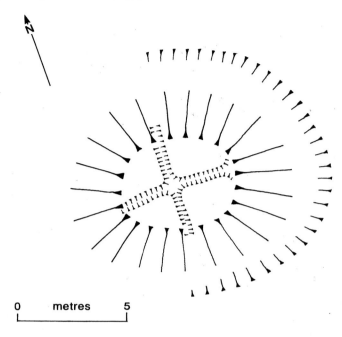

0   metres   5

27. Plan of a segmented round pillow mound on Minchinhampton Common, Gloucestershire: the pattern of two lateral grooves, crossing in the centre, was christened the 'hot cross bun' form by O. G. S. Crawford.

mounds have often been confused with other forms of field monument – several have been excavated in the belief that they were round barrows, and in the absence of excavation it can, indeed, be difficult to say for sure whether an example associated with a group of rectangular mounds is an earlier barrow or a circular pillow mound. There is also the possibility of confusing the larger examples with medieval mill mounds, which also often exhibit shallow surface grooves in the form of a cross, where the cross-trees of the mill were once buried.

The fact that many examples exhibit clear signs of segmenting suggests that round mounds were constructed for exactly the same reasons as rectangular ones, and post-medieval documents, such as an early seventeenth-century survey of the Duke of Hertford's park at Amesbury in Wiltshire, do indeed occasionally refer to 'round Coney berries'. But it is possible that some had a different purpose. At Y Foel in Powys a single circular mound occurs in a group otherwise composed entirely of mounds of normal rectangular form (at least fifty-four in all). In contrast

28. These artificial burrows, excavated within the hillfort at Danebury, are of unusual form. They consist of a slot, dug into the chalk at the base of a broader trench. From its sides, burrows were bored through the chalk, running diagonally to the surface. It is probable that the slots always lacked overlying mounds.

to the other excavated mounds, it displayed 'virtually no disturbance by rabbits' and contained no artificial burrows. Instead, the centre of the mound contained traces of 'an almost vertically-sided feature, resembling a posthole'. The excavator, Robert Silvester, suggested that it may have been raised to provide stability to a pole surmounted by a platform carrying a trap to catch birds of prey.

Warreners did not always construct mounds for the rabbits to live in: there were other ways of providing suitable accommodation. In a few warrens, artificial burrows were dug into the subsoil and simply covered over with wood or turfs, bringing them more or less flush with the land surface. At Mount Down in Hampshire, for example, aerial photographs revealed soil marks resembling four longhouses, with internal subdivisions, located within a prehistoric field system. Geophysical survey recorded strong magnetic anomalies, which were initially interpreted as masses of daub burnt *in situ*. This particular warren was clearly of no great antiquity, for excavation revealed that chicken wire was the real cause of the survey readings. It is possible that some of the artificial burrows excavated within the hillfort at Danebury similarly lacked overlying mounds (figure 28). Some took the form of a slot, excavated into the chalk at the base of a broader trench: from its sides, burrows were bored through the chalk, diagonally to the surface.

More common was the practice of using some existing earthwork for housing the rabbits. Many prehistoric earthworks have the name 'warren' applied to them, such as Warren Ring hillfort at Littlebury in Essex, while documentary and cartographic evidence makes it clear that the earthworks of deserted medieval villages, redundant castles or old salt-working mounds were all used as warrens. Such features might be altered by warreners in a host of ways, seemingly designed to confuse later archaeologists. The monument known as Cockmoor Dykes in Yorkshire comprises twenty closely spaced parallel banks and ditches which run along the Troutsdale escarpment, part of an extensive system of late prehistoric boundary earthworks that delineate large territories in the limestone uplands. But only the six largest dykes are actually prehistoric: the other fourteen seem to have been added in the eighteenth century when the area became a large warren. Long barrows or round barrows – alone or in groups – made ideal warrens and might be enclosed with a bank and a ditch, like the group at Winterbourne Stoke in Wiltshire, still helpfully described as 'The Coneygarth' on the 1:10,000 Ordnance Survey map. Artificial burrows were sometimes constructed within them, as in the case of Julliberrie's Grave long barrow in Kent, which in the nineteenth century displayed clear signs of 'segmenting'; or the cairn on Wigber Low in Derbyshire, excavated by John Collis, which had two stone-lined burrows inserted into it, probably during the nineteenth century.

On some warrens, banks of low-growing vegetation appear to have been established to shelter the rabbits. One example survives on the Ashridge estate in Hertfordshire, on the thin chalk soils of the Chiltern escarpment. A number of strips of box bushes about 15 metres wide – some planted on top of earlier lynchets – lie within an area called 'Box Warren' in a survey of 1656. The strips are shown, much as they are today, on an estate map of 1762. A manorial survey of Dorking in Surrey, drawn up in 1580, describes 'the lodge and warren of cunneys with a close grown with box containing 12 acres', while R. G. Haynes has described how Headland was unusual among the Dartmoor warrens in lacking pillow mounds 'due to the unique practice ... of accommodating rabbits in walled enclosures thickly planted with sheltering gorse ... the enclosures would have been practical and easy to net, varying in size as they do between a quarter and two acres.'

5
Boundaries and enclosures

Many warrens were enclosed, partly to protect the rabbits from predators but mainly to prevent them from straying on to neighbouring properties, where they might be lost to the warrener or cause damage to crops. Physical boundaries also helped define the legal area of the warren, making the prosecution of poachers more straightforward, and in some cases, perhaps, served as an expression of the wealth and status of the owner.

Where warrens abutted on areas of open heath or moor escape was probably not a major problem. Rabbits were generally loath to range far from their known territory, social group and good supplies of food, to seek their fortune in the bleak unknown, where they could do little damage anyway. But where warrens lay adjacent to arable land there were frequent problems, especially during drought conditions or when food ran short. As early as 1392 a colony of rabbits at Iken on the coastal heaths of Suffolk – descendants of escapees from Dunningworth warren, some 4 km to the west – caused serious damage to crops. There were also potential problems where warrens under different ownerships lay next to each other, as in the Plym valley on Dartmoor or in parts of the East Anglian Breckland, especially where each specialised in the production of different varieties of rabbit.

The problem of escape may have become more serious in the course of the seventeenth and eighteenth centuries, as stocking levels on warrens were increased, for in overcrowded conditions rabbits suffered from stress and were more likely to stray. While even the larger medieval warrens were often surrounded in whole or part by a bank, ditch or fence – a *fosse* is thus recorded at Lakenheath in Suffolk in the early fourteenth century – physical boundaries seem to have become more common, and more substantial, in the course of the post-medieval period.

In heathland and downland areas warrens were usually enclosed by banks of earth and turf, between 1 and 1.5 metres in height. These were topped with faggots of gorse, branches of blackthorn, or occasionally bundles of reeds, which overhung the inner face of the bank in order to prevent escape; or, more rarely, by live bushes of gorse or thorn, below a capping of turf. The inner face was sometimes lined with flint or other stones, to deter burrowing. Banks of this type could be extraordinarily wasteful of pasture: an example about 1.3 metres high might require as much as 24 square metres of turf to be stripped for every metre of its length. Many such banks originally had – and sometimes still have – a

29. One of the banks marking the south-western boundary of High Lodge Warren in the Suffolk Breckland, revealed by recent felling in a Forestry Commission plantation.

somewhat asymmetrical profile, with a fairly vertical face on the inside but a more sloping one on the outside of the warren. The remains of numerous examples can still be seen, albeit now in a much decayed state, in the East Anglian Breckland, running across heaths or (more usually) through Forestry Commission plantations (figure 29). The largest heathland warrens might be encompassed by banks more than 15 km in length (figure 30). Similar, but usually more compact, banks of turf and chalk were used to define some of the warrens in chalkland areas, as on the Lincolnshire Wolds or the Wessex Downs. As added security, warrens might be enclosed in whole or part by two or even more parallel banks, one often added at a later stage. Where, as happened in several places in the East Anglian Breckland, two warrens abutted there were sometimes three or four parallel banks running across the heath, as for example where the boundaries of Brandon Warren and High Lodge Warren ran next to each other for nearly a kilometre.

In upland areas drystone walls were usually employed, or more rarely revetted embankments. Some Cotswold warrens were also walled – like that on Bathampton Down near Bath. Walls provided better barriers to escape than earthen banks, and there was usually only a single perimeter wall, rather than the multiple banks often seen on lowland warrens. The walls were normally between 1.5 and 2.5 metres in height and in some

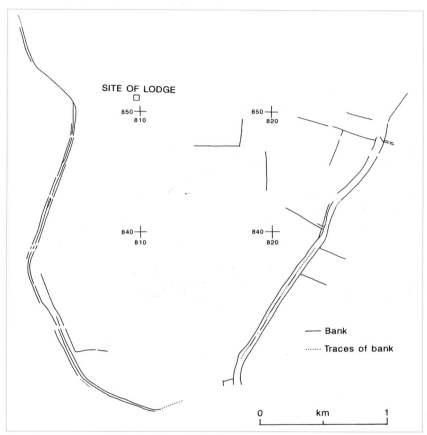

30. The boundary banks of High Lodge Warren, just outside Thetford in the Norfolk Breckland, are still a notable feature of the landscape, although they have been destroyed in places by later agriculture and forestry. The warren was bounded to the west by Brandon Warren and Wangford Warren, and to the east by Westwick Warren, which in part explains the multiple, complex character of its boundary banks.

cases – as at Wood Hall Warren, Carperby, in North Yorkshire (figure 31) – they had an overhanging coping, projecting from the wall face, to deter high-jumping escapees. Some warrens, such as those in the Tabular Hills of North Yorkshire, had boundaries of both types: turf or stone walls were used on the more level terrain, but stone walls alone on the sides of the valleys. Wire netting began to be employed on some warrens in the 1850s, usually in limited lengths to firm up particularly vulnerable boundaries. It was usually sunk into the ground to a depth of half a

31. The high boundary walls of Wood Hall Warren, Carperby, in Wensleydale, North Yorkshire, have an overhanging coping to deter escape.

metre or so, to prevent the rabbits from burrowing underneath.

As well as having purpose-built walls or banks, many warrens made use of other features, natural or man-made, in their circuits. Methwold Warren in Norfolk, for example, used the Dark Age linear earthwork known as the Fossditch as its western boundary, while Snainton Dyke on the Tabular Hills in North Yorkshire has a turf wall running along its crest: the two features together formed the eastern boundary of High Scamridge Warren. In upland areas especially, streams and rivers were often used as boundaries – rabbits have a considerable aversion to water. Most of the Dartmoor warrens included at least one stretch of natural watercourse along their perimeter.

Some warrens, as well as having perimeter walls or banks, also had internal subdivisions, defined by the same kinds of banks or walls which formed the outer boundary. A warren might be subdivided because more than one variety of rabbit was kept there, or because its area was also being used for keeping sheep or cattle and the meagre grazing needed to be managed carefully. More usually, subdivisions were made in order to allow portions of the warren to be ploughed and planted for a few years,

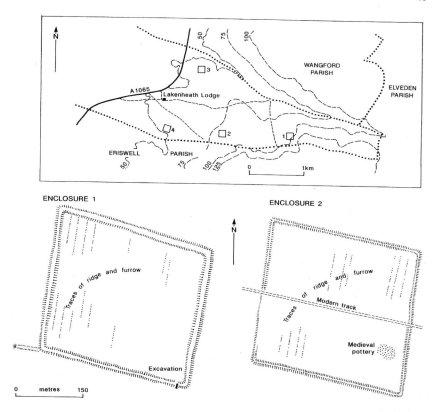

32. Enclosures on Lakenheath Warren in the Suffolk Breckland, defined by low earthwork banks, contain faint traces of ploughing and were probably used for the cultivation of fodder crops. (After C. Taylor)

before being returned to grass, in a form of 'convertible husbandry': this improved the quality of the sward, as well as providing extra fodder for the rabbits. Crops like turnips or swedes might also be cultivated in small, discrete enclosures within the warren. Good examples survive on Lakenheath Warren in the Suffolk Breckland: four enclosures, almost square in shape and each covering between 4 and 6 hectares (figure 32). They are surrounded by low banks around 0.6 metres in height, which lack any obvious entrances, and they contain slight plough-ridges, showing that they were once under cultivation. In upland areas such

33. The remains of the large nineteenth-century warren at Traianglas in Powys include, beside numerous well-defined pillow mounds, a number of enclosures; some contain plough-ridges and were presumably used to cultivate fodder crops.

fodder plots were enclosed with stone walls, as at Ystradfellte and Traianglas in the Brecon Beacons, Powys (figure 33).

Root crops and hay were not the only fodder used by the warreners, especially in the period before the late seventeenth century. Young bracken and other 'rowe', or coarse grass, were used; dandelions and groundsel might be specially cultivated; and branches were cut from pollards or coppices to provide 'leafy hay' and also – when laid on top of the mounds – to give the rabbits extra protection from the elements. A lease for the warren at Knebworth in Hertfordshire, dating from 1722, thus allowed the tenant 'once in every yeare' during the twenty-one year

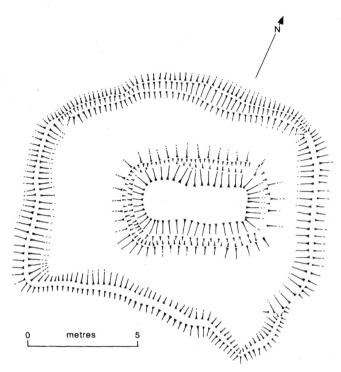

34. A sub-rectangular enclosure surrounding a pillow mound at Llanfair Clydogau in Ceredigion. Such enclosures were probably intended to give special protection to breeding does and young rabbits living in 'clappers'. (After David Austin)

lease 'to Lopp sixty Pollards for Browse for the Rabbitts'. Hazel, elder and ash were especially favoured and on the Mount Misery warren in North Yorkshire coppiced stools of ash and hazel still survive, growing from the tops of stone walls, presumably to offer some protection from the rabbits.

One last class of enclosure needs to be briefly mentioned. At a number of places rectangular, sub-rectangular or circular enclosures, defined by banks or walls, surround single mounds, or small groups of mounds, of round or rectangular form, as at Llanfair Clydogau in Ceredigion (figure 34), Friarhead near Flashby in North Yorkshire and Wanborough in Wiltshire. These enclosures were perhaps intended to give special protection to breeding does and young rabbits living in 'clapper' mounds, particularly vulnerable to predators, and it is possible that in some cases the enclosure itself (rather than the mounds within it) was termed a 'clapper'. In 1551 the lord of the manor of Sevenhampton in Wiltshire thus described how he had made 'vii or eight severall berryes in Clappers' on a disputed area of land. It is noticeable that such enclosed mounds can occur in warrens where pillow mounds of normal, unenclosed form are completely absent, as at Knettishall in Suffolk, and that they are often found close to the warren lodge, as probably at Llanfair Clydogau, presumably reflecting the particular attention that needed to be paid to the breeding does and their young.

6
Tip traps and vermin traps

Rabbits were usually caught on the warren by using some combination of dogs, nets and ferrets. A long net (or 'hay') might be erected between the rabbits and their burrows, and the animals driven into it by dogs, usually lurchers or tumblers. Alternatively, ferrets might be introduced into the burrows, and the bolting rabbits caught in nets placed at the various entrances. Both methods, as we have seen, were considerably facilitated by the construction of pillow mounds. But on some warrens the rabbits were caught in *types* or tip traps.

Many examples survive on the Tabular Hills in North Yorkshire, on former moorland now buried beneath Forestry Commission plantations. They take the form of circular pits, a metre deep and around a metre in diameter, which are lined with dry-stone walling and slope outwards towards the base. Most are located beside the perimeter bank or dry-stone wall of an enclosure, which might range in size from 5 or 6 metres square to as much as a hectare (figures 35 and 36). A narrow wooden

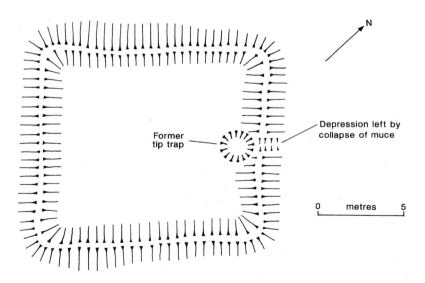

35. The remains of a small 'type' or tip trap enclosure in Dalby Forest, North Yorkshire. The turf walls are now represented only by low earthworks, but the position of the 'muce', and of the tip trap itself, are still clear.

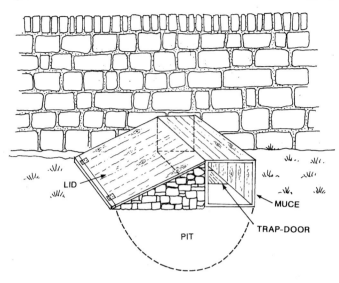

36. Diagram of a typical tip trap. A narrow wooden tunnel or *muce* runs through the wall and across the top of the pit: here there is a small trap-door in the tunnel floor, which is wedged shut for a time so that the rabbits can reach fodder. When the wedges are removed the rabbits fall into the pit, from which they can be removed via the larger wooden trap-door. (After A. Harris and D. A. Spratt)

37. Tip trap set against an internal wall on Wood Hall Warren, Carperby, North Yorkshire.

tunnel, called a *muce*, ran through the wall or bank and across the top of the pit, where there was a trap-door in the tunnel floor. For much of the time this was kept wedged shut, allowing the rabbits to use the muce as a way of getting from one side of the barrier to the other, attracted in by the provision of suitable fodder. When the wedges were removed, large numbers would be caught, the rabbits usually surviving the short fall alive. A larger wooden covering to the pit prevented any escape: this could be easily removed when the rabbits were extracted.

Such traps were mainly a feature of the north-east of England. They are found not only in the Tabular Hills and on the North Yorkshire Moors, but on warrens in the eastern Pennines, most notably at Wood Hall Warren at Carperby (figure 37), and they were once common on the Lincolnshire Wolds. Here, the types were normally placed in particularly small enclosures, each around 4 metres square, defined by turf walls. In August, September and October the rabbits were enticed into the enclosure with generous supplies of fodder, and the trap was kept shut. But in November the catch was released, and as many as four hundred rabbits were taken at a time.

Outside the north-east of England tip traps were more rarely used. A few are known from the warrens on the Brecon Beacons, as at Traianglas, Cray and Ystradfellte, although these were often rather larger than those on the Tabular Hills, up to 3 metres in diameter and usually tapering towards the base rather than the top. Again, they were set within small enclosures. Those at Ystradfellte were quadrilateral in shape, 20 metres in length, 13 metres wide at one end and tapering to 6 metres at the other. Tip traps were also introduced into at least two Breckland warrens, Thetford and Santon Downham, in the nineteenth century. Here they were circular, around 3 metres deep, and lined with chalk and flint: no evidence of their existence seems to survive today beneath the Forestry Commission pine plantations. Unlike other examples, these were located in the open and their iron lids were covered with hay, on which the rabbits would be encouraged to feed.

Tip traps were probably a relatively recent development in the long history of warrening. Most of the Yorkshire and Lincolnshire warrens in which they are found appear to have originated in the eighteenth or nineteenth centuries, while the Welsh examples are all apparently of nineteenth-century date. It is noteworthy that William Marshall, writing in 1788, described tip trapping as a 'more modern' method of catching rabbits than the use of nets. Tip traps may have become feasible only as the stocking levels on warrens were increased through the use of fodder crops. Certainly, one early twentieth-century observer suggested that the method had been adopted only on those Breckland warrens where rabbits were 'so abundant as to render it practicable'. It is also noteworthy that while tip traps can be found in some warrens which were equipped with pillow mounds, as in south Wales, they are more characteristic of warrens which lacked them, such as those on the Tabular Hills. Pillow mounds, as we have seen, were probably constructed as much to aid trapping as to provide accommodation, and where they were employed warreners were perhaps reluctant to go to the effort of digging tip traps as well.

Other kinds of trap were constructed on warrens not to take rabbits but rather to catch the various vermin – principally weasels, rats and stoats –

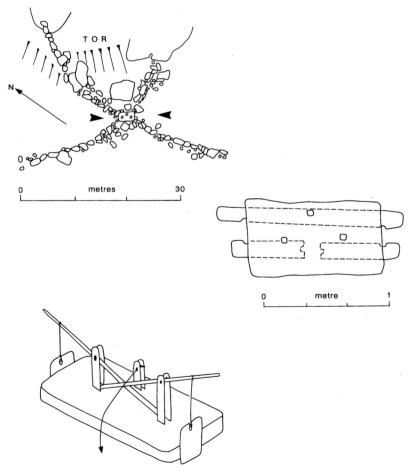

38. Remains of a stone vermin trap on Dartmoor (top), detail of the trap lid (centre) and reconstruction of the trip mechanism (bottom). (After R. Haynes)

that preyed upon them. In most cases these were made of wood and have left no direct archaeological trace, although they are illustrated in a number of eighteenth-century gamekeeping manuals. But on Dartmoor warrens stone versions were constructed, and many of these survive *in situ*, albeit in fragmentary form. They were built of five large flat stones. A heavy rectangular base stone, placed flush with the turf, supported three uprights: one ran the full length of the trap; the others, which were smaller, formed the opposite side, leaving a gap in the centre (figure 38). A heavy flat cap stone completed what was, in effect, a square-sectioned tunnel of stone with openings at either end, and in the middle of one side. The side opening held a trip mechanism; the ends could be closed by pieces of slate which, held in grooves in the side stones, could be dropped and lifted with relative ease. The cover stones have two or more holes drilled in them, usually 3.8 cm in diameter and the same deep. These seem to have held upright wooden posts that were connected, by wire or string, to the slate shutters closing the trap. When a stoat or weasel ran through the 'tunnel' it would step on a plate that was connected to a trigger passing through the side slate. This released a small block of stone to which were attached the other ends of the strings. The slate shutters, no longer held up by the string or wire, would fall under their own weight, thus trapping the unfortunate predator.

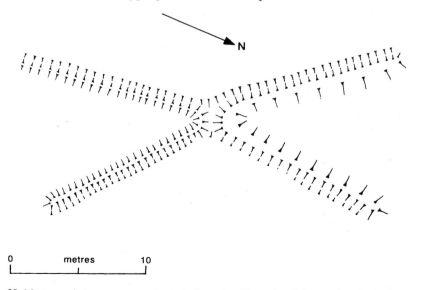

0   metres   10

39. Most vermin traps were constructed of wood and have thus left no archaeological traces, although their low funnel walls sometimes remain, as here at Llanfair Clydogau, Ceredigion. (After David Austin)

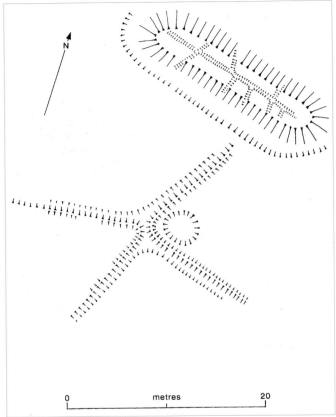

40. The
characteristic
opposed chevrons
marking the site
of a vermin trap
beside a
segmented pillow
mound on
Minchinhampton
Common,
Gloucestershire.
The pit beside the
trap is a later
feature.

The traps were usually unbaited and the animals were encouraged to
enter them by low funnel walls, of stone and earth, seldom more than
0.6 metres in height. These were arranged as two opposed Vs, with the
trap positioned in the small gap between them. Traps, and funnel walls,
were carefully placed so as to intercept natural access routes to the warren
and its denizens and they usually made use of large natural or man-made
obstructions, such as stone outcrops or ancient walls, to help channel the
course of the predator.

Large numbers of stone vermin traps have been recorded on the
Dartmoor warrens. They are probably of seventeenth- and eighteenth-
century date: R. G. Haynes, who made a detailed study of them, suggested
that they fell out of use in the course of the eighteenth century as a result
of the widespread adoption of the gin trap and the shotgun. The wooden

41. The low earthworks of a vermin trap on Minchinhampton Common.

counterparts constructed on warrens in other areas have left no direct archaeological traces, although they are often referred to in leases. Perh Kalm, a Swedish tourist who came to England in 1748, described traps which he had seen in some Hertfordshire warrens and which he thought were for catching rabbits but were almost certainly intended to trap predators. They were constructed of 'four boards, like a long box. At each end hangs a perpendicular board, like a door, which by specially contrived arrangement above the trap ... can be hoisted up so that the entrance stands open. In the middle of the trap an iron pin or a little wooden rod goes cross-wise.' When this was pressed down, 'a pin on the outside slips loose and the boards at both ends fall down'.

While wooden traps like these have not themselves survived, indirect evidence for their existence sometimes remains in the form of the cross-shaped arrangements of stones and/or earth created to funnel the vermin towards them. At Llanfair Clydogau in Ceredigion, for example, three such features were found by David Austin and his team, each consisting of two chevrons laid apex to apex but separated by a narrow (about 1 metre wide) area of flat ground, where the trap would have been positioned (figure 39). At least one similar feature exists on Minchinhampton Common in Gloucestershire, again consisting of two opposed chevrons defined by low (about 0.2 metre) earth banks, this time about 0.5 metre apart (at SO 8547000938: figures 40 and 41). Many other examples of such slight earthworks doubtless remain to be discovered.

7
Warren houses and lodges

Warren houses, or lodges, provided accommodation for the warrener and a place to keep carcasses and skins, as well as all the nets, traps and other necessary equipment. Not all warrens had them. Where small warrens were established on open commons or lay close to a mansion, they were usually absent. But they were indispensable on the larger, commercial warrens. Here they were a particularly noticeable feature of the landscape, standing alone in the empty, windswept expanse of the close-cropped turf – so much so, indeed, that they became an image of solitary isolation. In Shakespeare's *Much Ado about Nothing* Claudio is described as being 'as lonely as a lodge in a warren'.

Few medieval warren lodges survive. The best-preserved is that at Thetford in the East Anglian Breckland, erected by the Prior of Thetford to serve Westwick Warren in the early fifteenth century and currently under the care of English Heritage (figure 42). What we see today is the shell of the medieval core, stripped of later accretions by a fire in 1935. It is reminiscent of a small castle: a well-built tower house, 8.5 by 5.7

42. The fine fifteenth-century warren lodge at Thetford in Norfolk. As well as serving to house carcasses and equipment and providing accommodation for the warrener, this elaborate building may also have been used by its owner, the Prior of Thetford, while on recreational hunting trips.

metres in plan, constructed of local flint with some brick and limestone dressings. It had two floors, each with a single room, connected by a staircase in the south-west corner. The upper floor was used as accommodation for the warrener, the lower provided storage for carcasses, skins and equipment. Both floors had a fireplace, that on the lower presumably to provide the heat necessary for drying skins. The building was clearly designed with serious defence in mind. It has small windows, with those on the ground floor narrower than those above – little more than arrow slits – while above the single entrance is a *meurtrière*, a hole for dropping missiles on attackers. These features indicate the high value of rabbit skins and the fact that attacks from armed intruders were expected, although to some extent the building may also have served as an expression of the power and status of its owner. It is also probable that, like the lodges found in medieval deer parks, the building sometimes served as a base for recreational hunting. Rabbits were not highly prized as game in the Middle Ages but they were not entirely neglected as a quarry, and the lodge was conveniently located only a short distance (about 2.5 km) to the north-west of Thetford Priory.

The lodge at Mildenhall in Suffolk, some 14 km to the south-west, is slightly later in date and broadly similar in form, if rather less impressive. It has been extensively repaired under the auspices of the Friends of Thetford Forest and the Forestry Commission, with Heritage Lottery Fund support. It is another flint tower house, 6.4 by 7.5 metres in plan and again with two floors (figure 43). These had been thought to be the only warren lodges to survive in Breckland – together with the masonry stump which is all that remains of Langford Warren lodge in Ickburgh. Research by Anne Mason has, however, revealed that fragments of several others – at Methwold, Lakenham, Eriswell and Santon – also remain, incorporated into later cottages or farm buildings. The need to protect the stock of the warren from poachers presumably explains why most of these buildings were constructed in commanding positions, with wide views across the surrounding landscape.

Outside East Anglia few medieval lodges remain. Norton Tower at Rylstone in North Yorkshire is another late medieval tower house, now reduced to a ruined single storey. It apparently served primarily as a deer park lodge, providing accommodation for the park keeper, and for its owner while on recreational hunting trips. But it lay at the centre of a warren (several pillow mounds remain around it) and it thus presumably also functioned as a base for warrening activity. The function of park lodge and warren house may well have been combined at other places, given the fact that warrens were often located within parks. Indeed, this kind of functional combination continued sporadically into the post-

43. Mildenhall Warren Lodge, Suffolk.

medieval period: at Ewden Cote on the Broomhead Hall estate to the north of Sheffield in the late eighteenth century the lodge provided shelter for shooting parties, as well as accommodation for the warrener and his family. It contained two chambers on the south side, one above the other, with fireplaces for drying skins.

Perhaps the most dramatic instance of combining working lodge with place of elite recreation is the unusual building erected in the 1590s at Rushton in Northamptonshire by the wealthy Catholic recusant Sir Thomas Tresham (figures 44 and 45). This was located within the rabbit warren a short distance from Rushton Hall and, as noted in Chapter 1, was a place for meditation and retreat, loaded with symbolism relating both to Tresham's name and to his belief in the Trinity and the Tridentine mass. The building thus has three sides, each 33 feet (10 metres) long and with three gables, three storeys and a three-sided chimney, and featured numerous similar numerical references and allusions in its structure and ornamentation. But the building is nevertheless referred to as the 'Warryners Lodge' in the estate accounts and clearly served as a working warren house. Typically, it had a single room on each floor,

44. Sir Thomas Tresham's unique three-sided warren lodge at Rushton, Northamptonshire.

reached by a spiral staircase inserted into one of the corners. A half-basement provided a suitable place for storing carcasses. On each floor the corners of the triangle are sealed off as separate chambers, so that the main room is hexagonal in plan: the multiplicity of storage spaces thus created perhaps allowed rapid conversion from working lodge to place of retreat and meditation.

In some places flamboyant and elaborate lodges continued to be constructed well into the seventeenth century. Warren Cottage, which stands next to the group of pillow mounds in Hatfield Forest in Essex, was built in the 1680s. It is a small building, 9 metres by 4, originally with the customary single room on each floor connected by an external stair turret (figure 46). This latter feature, together with the elaborate patterned brickwork and massive external stack, gives the impression of wealth displayed in a flamboyant but somewhat archaic form. Perhaps its builder, Sir Edward Turnor – who was attempting to revive the warren here after a period of disuse – was keen to assert what he saw as his traditional rights in symbolic form over those of his litigious commoners.

Buildings like this were exceptional, however. Most post-medieval

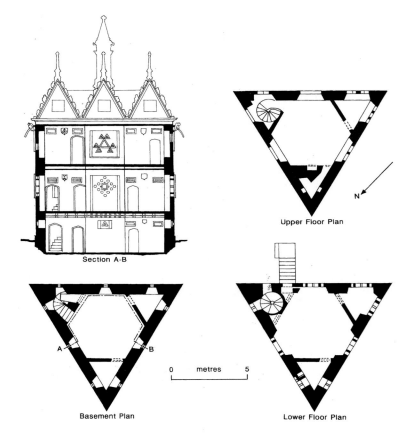

45. Plan and elevation of the Triangular Lodge at Rushton in Northamptonshire. (After RCHME)

warren houses were rather plain and functional in character, much like ordinary cottages or small farmhouses. Many of those which remain as ruins or wall bases on upland warrens were simple longhouses, while earthwork remains elsewhere suggest diminutive structures, such as the small cottage platform, 14 metres by 9 metres, associated with the pillow mound group at Lydiard Millicent in Wiltshire. At Danebury in Hampshire the site of the warren house was excavated as part of the wider examination of the hillfort interior: the excavator, Barry Cunliffe, described it as 'a simple affair built of cob walls on a flint and cob base...

46. Warren Cottage, Hatfield Forest, Essex, was built as a warren lodge in the 1680s.

The floor was of flint rubble. There was little evidence of comfort ...'.

In some areas, as on the Tabular Hills, it was usual to sell the rabbits to middlemen immediately after capture, and so no special buildings or facilities were required for storing carcasses. But even where such buildings existed they have usually been rendered unrecognisable by subsequent alterations. On the later warrens especially some outbuildings might be provided for storing turnips and other fodder, but these are not obviously different from the structures erected on small farms in the eighteenth or nineteenth centuries. As a result, in most cases post-medieval warren houses, where they survive, proclaim their former function – if at all – only through their name, although even this can be misleading. 'Warren Farm' can just as easily refer to a building erected on a new site after a warren was destroyed, or even to a farm which existed close to a warren. The identity of the lodge for the vast warren at Minchinhampton in Gloucestershire is revealed by the name attached to the public house in the middle of the common: the Old Lodge (figure 47).

One intriguing mystery concerns the way in which, on several of the larger warrens, there are two or more separate lodges. Lakenheath Warren in the East Anglian Breckland, for example, had – by the early nineteenth

47. The lodge for Minchinhampton warren is now a public house but still bears an appropriate name – the Old Lodge. The tall central block probably represents the original lodge building.

century – a Lodge, a building called the Grotto Lodge, and a Warren House. On large warrens like this it may have been necessary to have more than one individual located close to the coneys, to keep watch over them: the buildings always seem to have been placed some distance from one another, in such a way as to allow maximum visibility across the landscape.

8
Conclusion

It will be apparent from this short survey that rabbit warrens have a distinctive archaeology which is important both in its own right and also for the potential confusion it can cause to field archaeologists. There is no doubt that many more pillow mounds remain to be discovered through careful field survey, and it is likely that others remain wrongly classified, as barrows or other archaeological features. Many kilometres of warren banks, and perimeter wall, survive in the landscape, neglected and unrecognised, and many more vermin traps and 'types' await discovery and proper recording. Above all, early lodges and warren houses may prove to have survived in greater numbers than it currently appears, incorporated into later buildings. All in all, there is a rich field of enquiry here for the field archaeologist and landscape historian, both amateur and professional.

9
Places to visit

Pillow mounds are widely distributed across England and Wales, often on common land. Many are shown on the 1:25,000 and often on the 1:50,000 Ordnance Survey maps, where they are identified in the customary gothic lettering employed to denote antiquities. They are often relatively uninspiring features: the largest concentrations, and those associated with other relics of warrening activity, make for the most rewarding visits.

The large group of mounds at **High Beach**, Epping Forest, Essex (TQ 411984) is easily reached from the M25 and, although suffering from some erosion, is still impressive. The twenty-six mounds in **Hatfield Forest**, also in Essex (TL 536199), are also worth visiting, not least because of their setting (within one of the finest surviving areas of wood-pasture in eastern England) and the fact that they have been created, in part, from an earlier earthwork. Warren Cottage, the former lodge, is private but can be viewed from a distance. Also easily reached, on open common land, are the group at **Ashley Down**, north-west of Sandown on the Isle of Wight (SZ 578876), and the three large concentrations on **Rockford Common** near Ellingham in Hampshire (SU 170086). The group at **Chirbury** in Shropshire (SO 304987) includes a fine cross-shaped example.

Among the many single mounds and small groups, attention should be drawn to those at **Crowborough** and **Forest Row** in the Ashdown Forest, East Sussex (TQ 404321 and TQ 494324), which are conveniently located close to public car parks, and which are good examples of the particularly long mounds that are characteristic of this part of England (the former also includes a good example of a V-shaped mound).

Typical examples of the often confusing association of pillow mounds with earlier earthworks can be seen at the hillforts at **Pilsdon Pen** in Dorset (ST 413031), **Dolebury** in Somerset (ST 450590) and **Croft Ambrey** in Herefordshire (SO 445665). At **Alton Barnes** in Wiltshire a pillow mound runs between two round barrows (SU 115637), while a short walk away two probable examples have been built into the sides of the Adam's Grave long barrow (SU 113634).

One of the most impressive pillow mound groups in lowland England – a veritable Mecca for the enthusiast – is that on **Minchinhampton Common** in Gloucestershire (SO 850015). Here there are around forty mounds, including a number of circular examples, many of which exhibit particularly clear signs of 'segmenting' – that is, the troughs formed by collapsed burrows built into the body of the mound. The Old Lodge public house is conveniently located in the middle of the common, with the earthworks of a vermin trap just to the north of its access drive.

None of these lowland groups, however, really compares with the impressive remains of the Dartmoor warrens, especially those at the upper end of the Plym valley: **Ditsworthy, Hentor, Willings Walls, Trowlesworthy** and **Legistor** (centred on SX 580650). Here, on open moorland with unrestricted access, the visitor can see innumerable pillow mounds of typical high-backed 'upland' form, and – with diligence – can find examples of the stone vermin traps for which the Dartmoor warrens are noted. Many of the Welsh warrens can also be approached on open moorland: particularly impressive are the large numbers of high-backed mounds, and associated enclosures and tip traps, at **Ystradfellte** (SN 890130). In the north of England, a number of groups can likewise be viewed on open moorland, a short distance off marked footpaths, including those at **Rathmell** (SD 793616) and **Hutton-le-Hole** (SE 695905). Especially striking are the groups at **Ravenstonedale** and **Waitby** (NY 718054 and NY 724061), which can be reached from the same footpath.

On the **Ashridge** estate in north-west Hertfordshire – at SP 965158, a short walk from the public car park for Ivinghoe Beacon, and on National Trust land – lies Box Warren, where the wide strips of box used to shelter the rabbits can still be seen.

The Breckland warrens, on the Norfolk–Suffolk border near Thetford, are also worth visiting. The area is now largely planted up by the Forestry Commission but the warren lodges at **Thetford** (TL 839841) and **Mildenhall** (TL 735755) are both carefully preserved and displayed. Particularly good stretches of multiple warren bank can be seen in the area around the High Lodge visitor centre (TL 811851), especially around TL 803846. The warrens on the **Tabular Hills** in North Yorkshire are also now mostly under conifer plantations but examples of 'types', set in their characteristic enclosures, can be found with some difficulty within Dalby Forest. Much more easily reached is Wood Hall Warren at **Carperby**, in the Yorkshire Dales (SD 985895). Public footpaths running through the area allow the high warren walls to be viewed, as well as a number of 'types', positioned beside the various internal walls.

In a class of its own is Sir Thomas Tresham's strange triangular warren lodge at **Rushton** in Northamptonshire (SP 830831), which is in the care of English Heritage and open to the public.

10
Further reading

Many of the excavations, surveys and discussions of pillow mounds and other aspects of the archaeology of rabbit warrens are buried away in obscure local archaeological and historical journals. More accessible, or of particular interest, are the following:

Austin, D. 'Excavations and survey at Bryn Cysegrfan, Llanfair Clydogau, Dyfed', *Medieval Archaeology*, 23 (1979), 130–65.

Bailey, M. 'The rabbit and the medieval East Anglian economy', *Agricultural History Review*, 36 (1988), 1–20.

Bettey, J. 'Origins of the Wiltshire rabbit industry', *Antiquaries Journal*, 84 (2004), 381–93.

Crawford, O. G. S. 'Barrows', *Antiquity*, 1 (1927), 431–2.

Cunliffe, B. *Danebury: An Iron Age Hill-fort in Hampshire*. Council for British Archaeology, London, 1984.

Gelling, P. 'Excavations at Pilsdon Pen 1964–1971', *Proceedings of the Prehistoric Society*, 43 (1977), 263–86.

Harris, A., and Spratt, D. A. 'The rabbit warrens of the Tabular Hills, North Yorkshire', *The Yorkshire Archaeological Journal*, 63 (1991), 177–98.

Haynes, R. G. 'Vermin traps and rabbit warrens on Dartmoor', *Post-Medieval Archaeology*, 4 (1970), 147–64.

Henderson, A. 'From coney to rabbit: the story of a managed coloniser', *The Naturalist*, 12 (1997), 101–21.

Lineham, C. D. 'Deserted sites and rabbit-warrens on Dartmoor, Devon', *Medieval Archaeology*, 10 (1966), 113–39.

Loveday, R., and Williamson, T. 'Rabbits or ritual? Artificial warrens and the Neolithic long mound tradition', *Archaeological Journal*, 145 (1988), 290–313.

Royal Commission on Ancient and Historical Monuments in Wales. *Glamorgan Volume III: Medieval Secular Monuments, Part II: Non-defensive*. HMSO, Cardiff, 1982.

Sheail, J. *Rabbits and Their History*. David & Charles, Newton Abbot, 1971.

Silvester, R. J. 'Pillow mounds at Y Foel, Llanllugan', *Montgomeryshire Collections*, 83 (1995), 75–90.

Stocker, D., and Stocker, M. 'Sacred profanity: the theology of rabbit breeding and the symbolic landscape of the warren', *World Archaeology*, 28 (1996), 265–72.

Tebbutt, C. F. 'Rabbit warrens in Ashdown Forest', *Sussex Notes and Queries*, 17 (1968), 12–17.

Williamson, T. 'Fish, fur and feather: man and nature in the post-medieval landscape', in K. Barker and T. Darvill (editors), *Making English Landscapes*. Bournemouth University School of Conservation Sciences Occasional Paper 3, 1997.

Index

Page numbers in italic refer to illustrations